IT'S TIME TO EAT A BLACKBERRY

It's Time to Eat a Blackberry

Walter the Educator

SKB
Silent King Books
A WhichHead Entertainment Imprint

Copyright © 2024 by Walter the Educator

All rights reserved. No part of this book may be reproduced in any manner whatsoever without written per- mission except in the case of brief quotations embodied in critical articles and reviews.

First Printing, 2024

Disclaimer

This book is a literary work; the story is not about specific persons, locations, situations, and/or circumstances unless mentioned in a historical context. Any resemblance to real persons, locations, situations, and/or circumstances is coincidental. This book is for entertainment and informational purposes only. The author and publisher offer this information without warranties expressed or implied. No matter the grounds, neither the author nor the publisher will be accountable for any losses, injuries, or other damages caused by the reader's use of this book. The use of this book acknowledges an understanding and acceptance of this disclaimer.

It's Time to Eat a Blackberry is a collectible early learning book by Walter the Educator suitable for all ages belonging to Walter the Educator's Time to Eat Book Series. Collect more books at WaltertheEducator.com

USE THE EXTRA SPACE TO TAKE NOTES AND DOCUMENT YOUR MEMORIES

BLACKBERRY

It's time to eat, come gather near,

It's Time to Eat a
Blackberry

A special fruit that's juicy and dear!

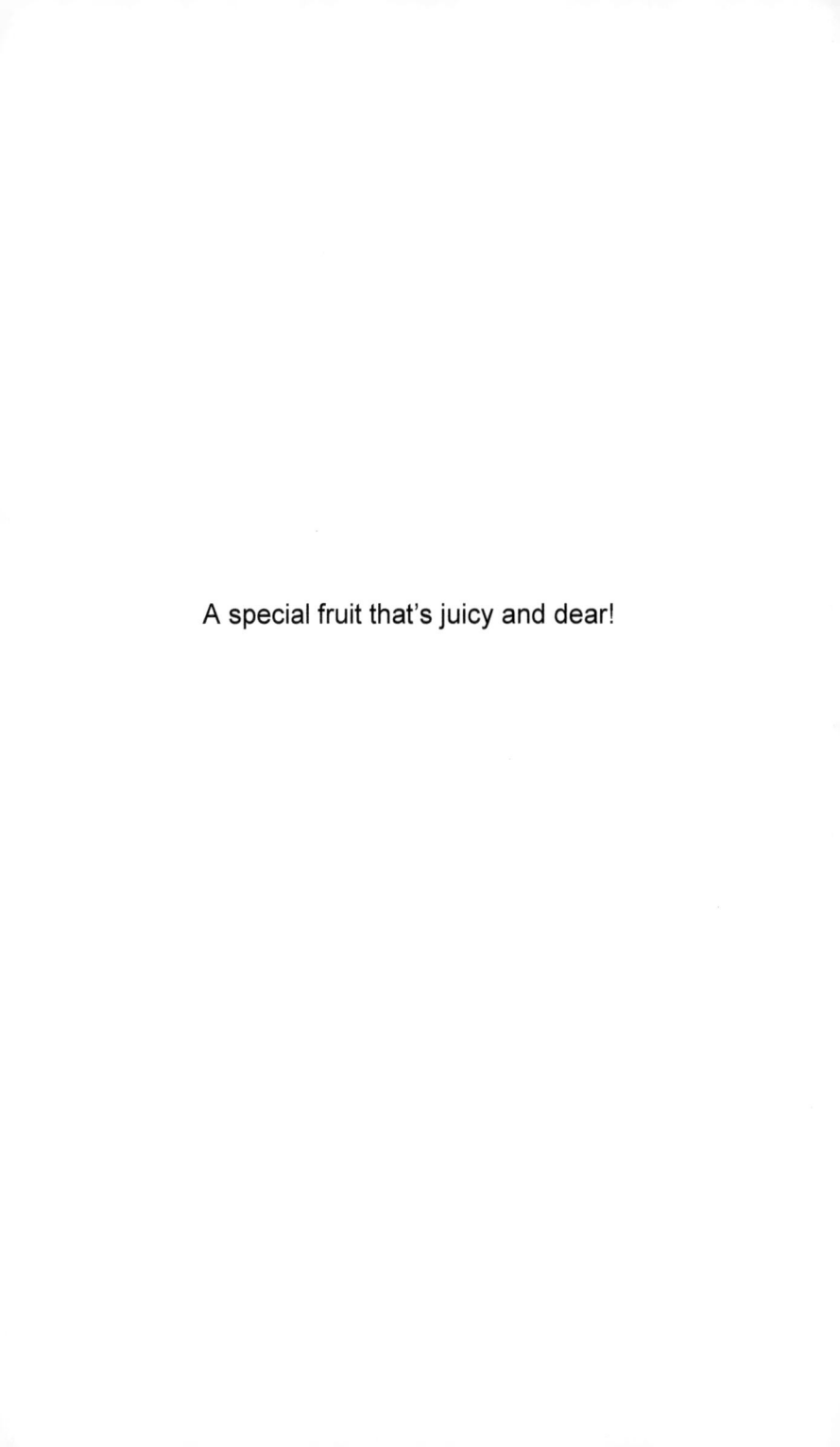

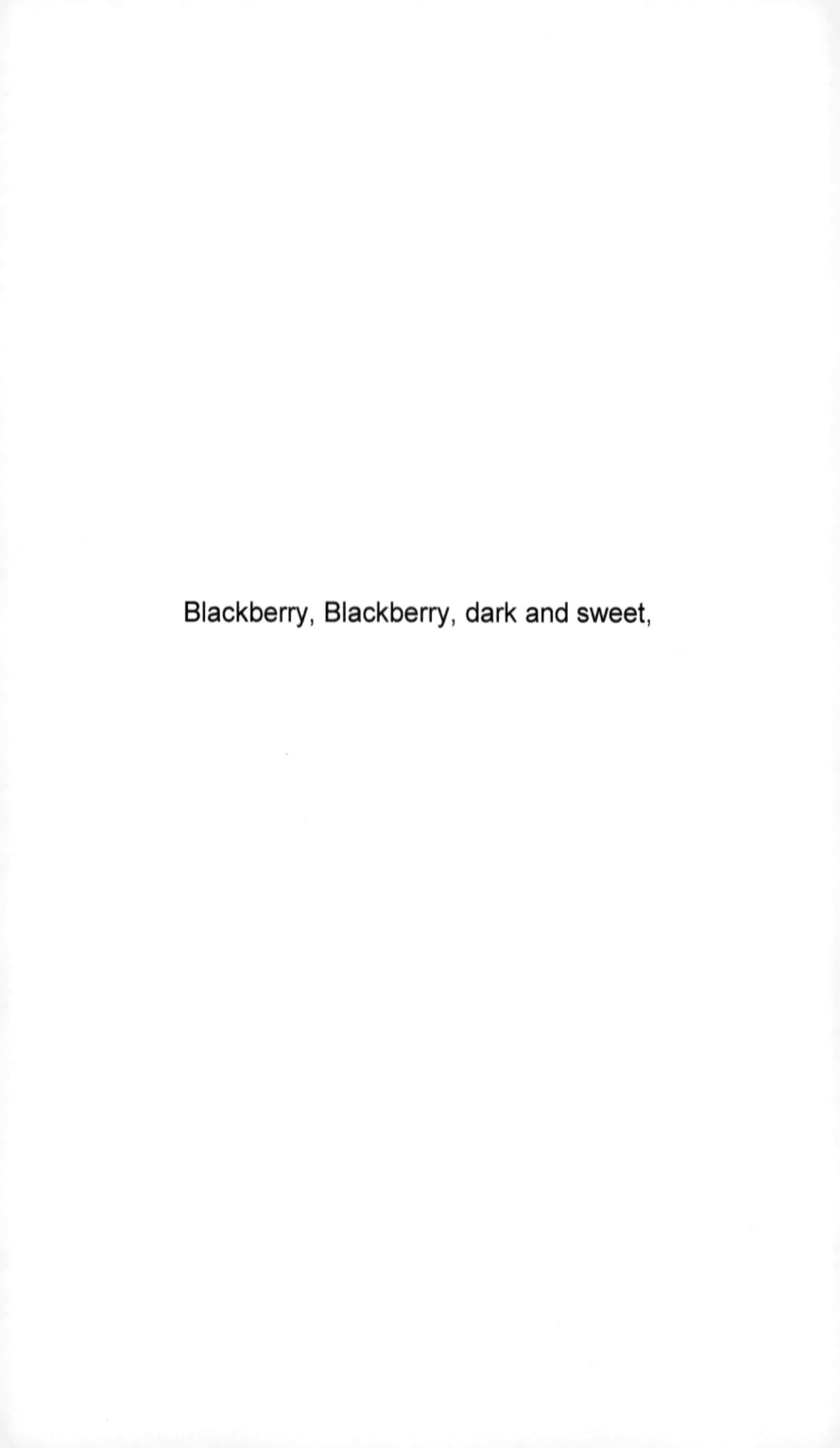

Blackberry, Blackberry, dark and sweet,

A little berry that's fun to eat!

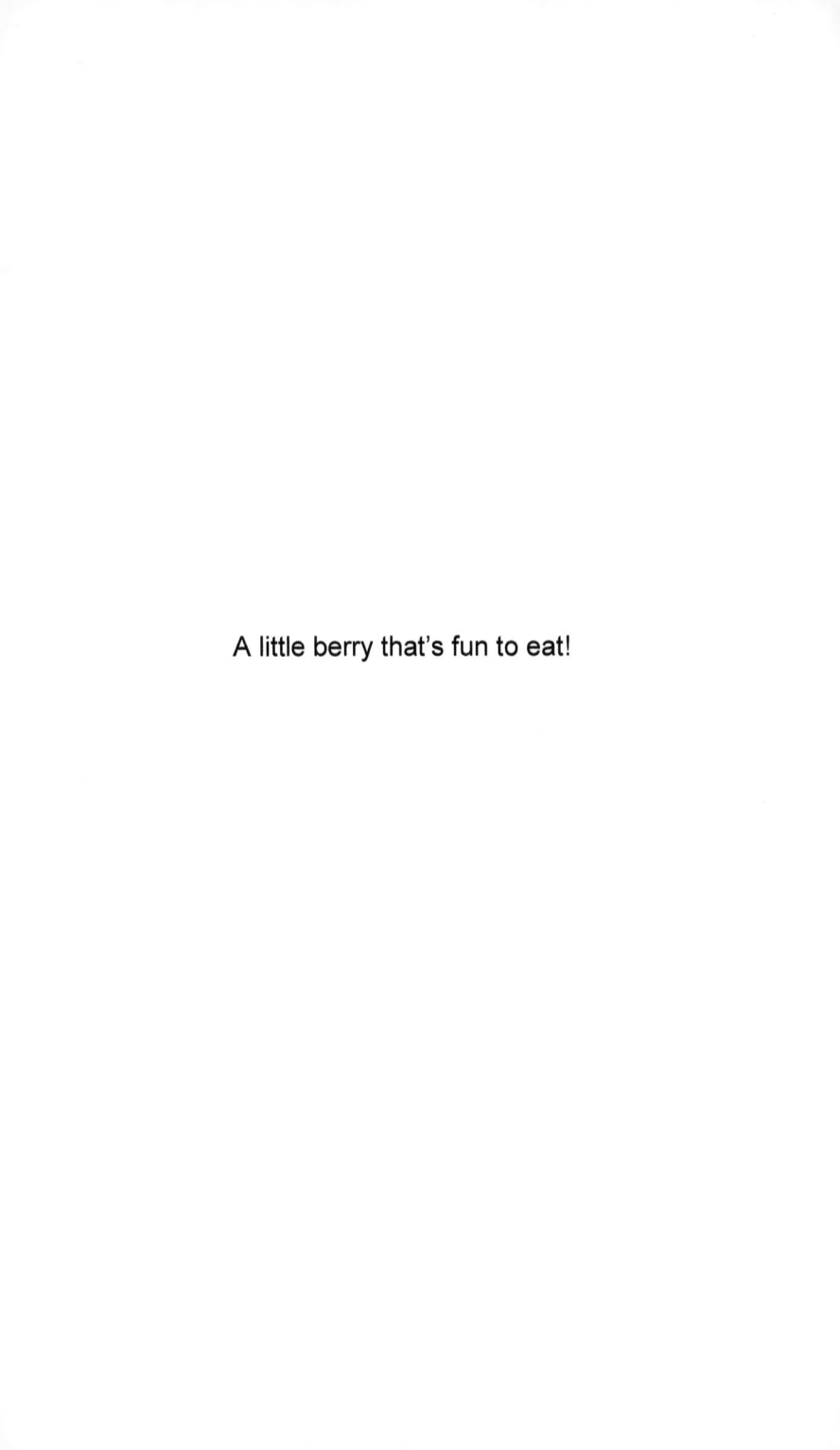

We pick them fresh, from bushes tall,

Black and shiny, they're not big at all.

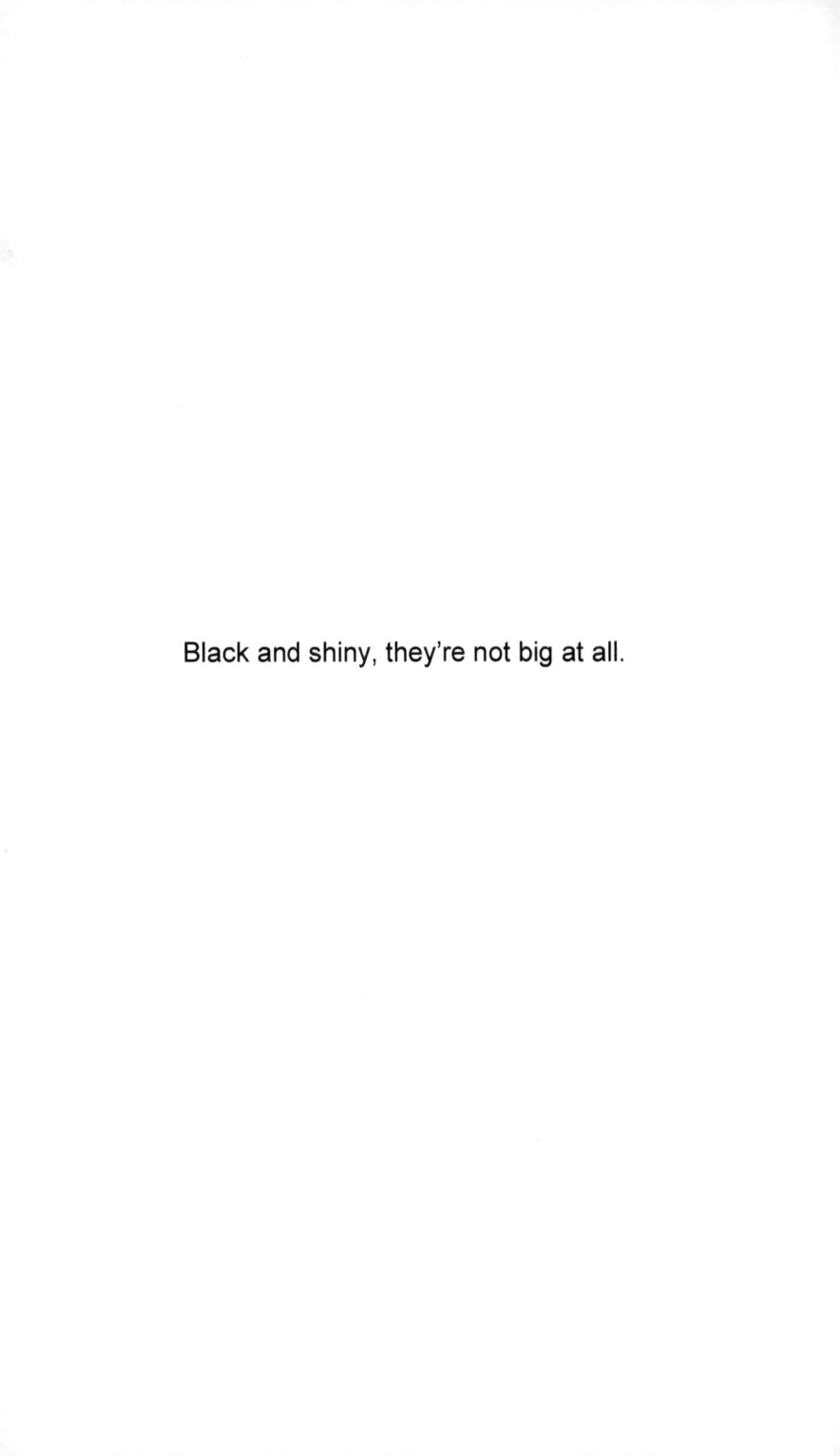

Round and plump, with bumpy skin,

Take a bite, and the fun begins!

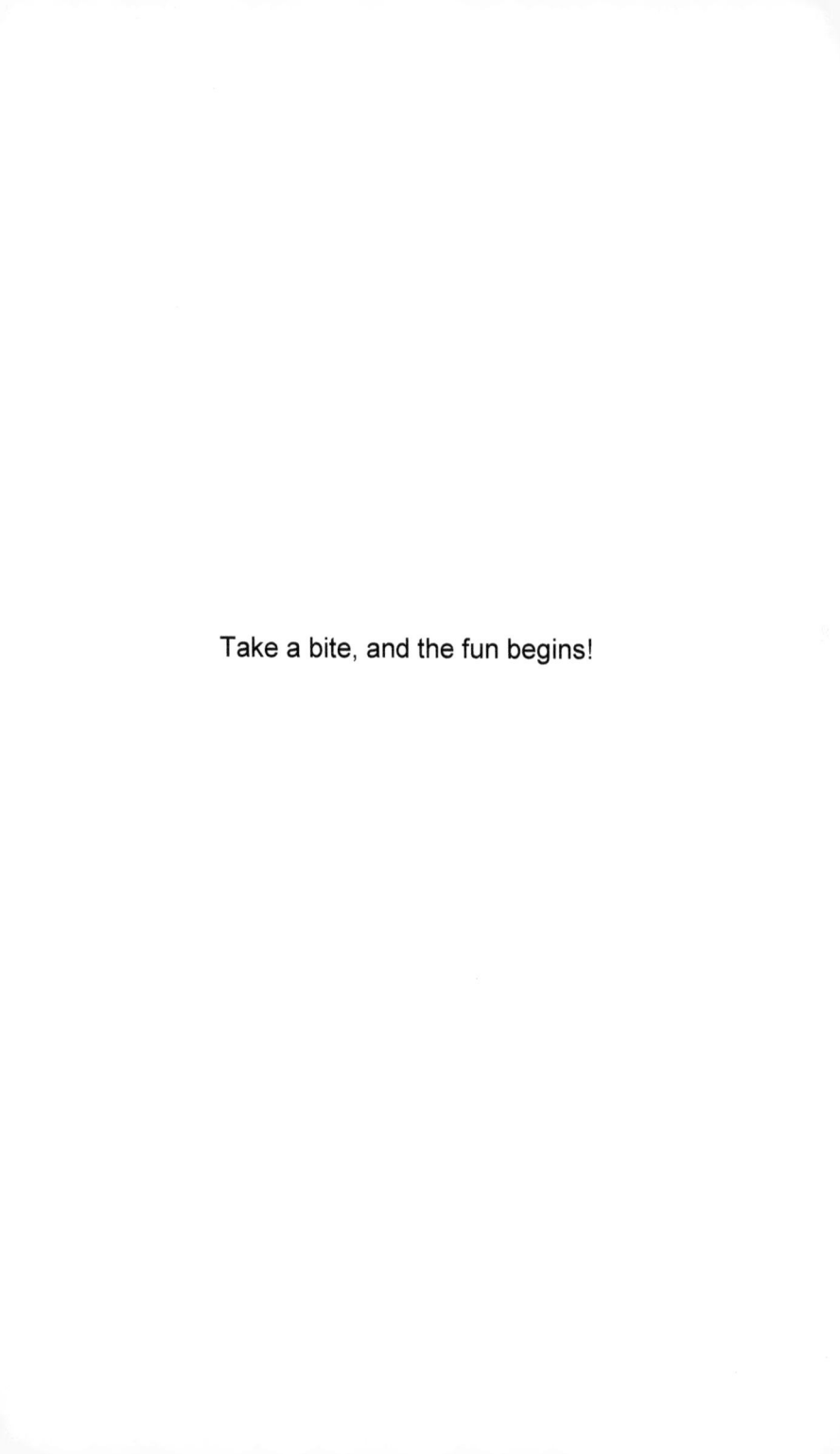

With every chew, the juice runs free,

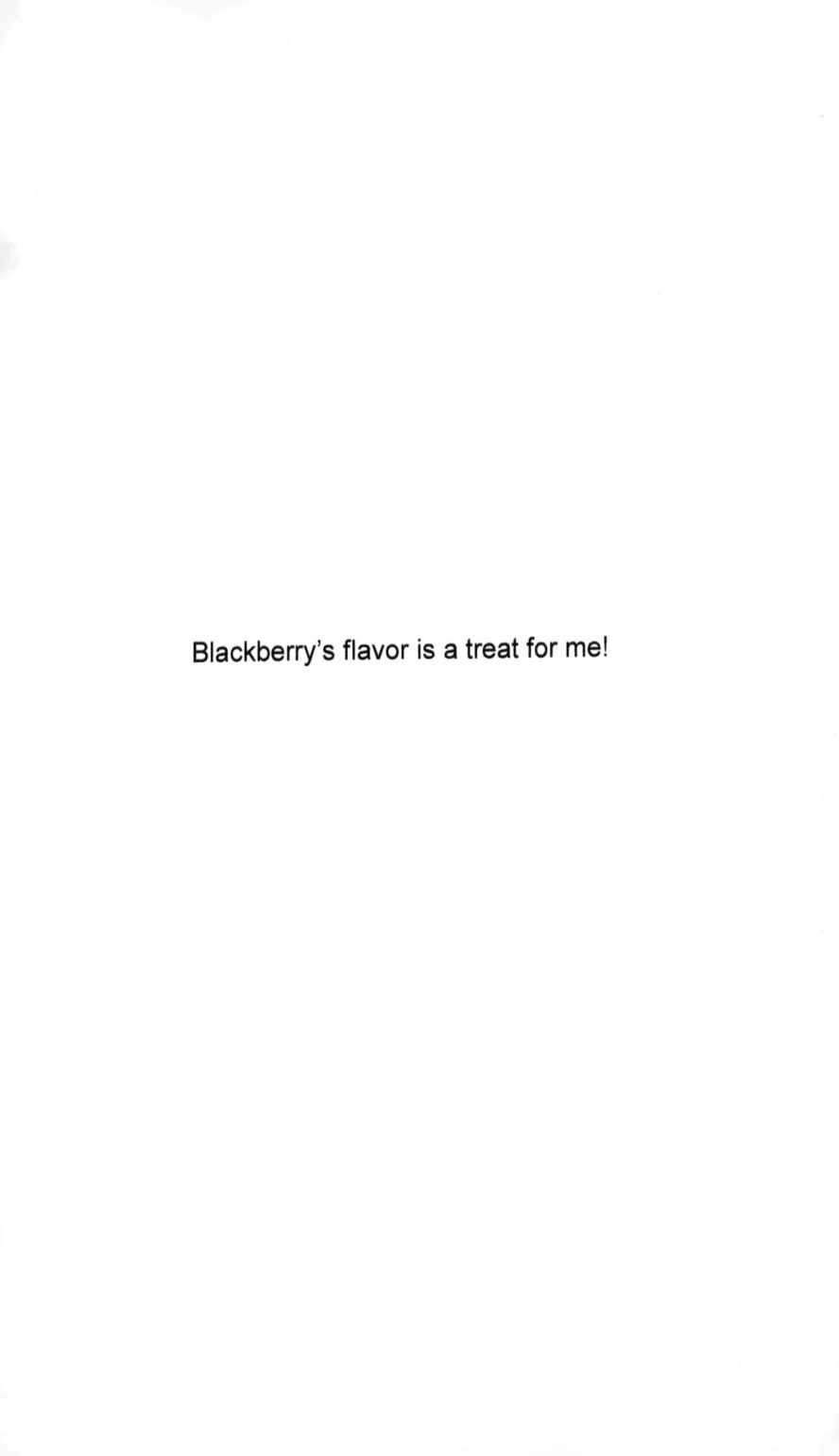

Blackberry's flavor is a treat for me!

A little bit tart, a little bit sweet,

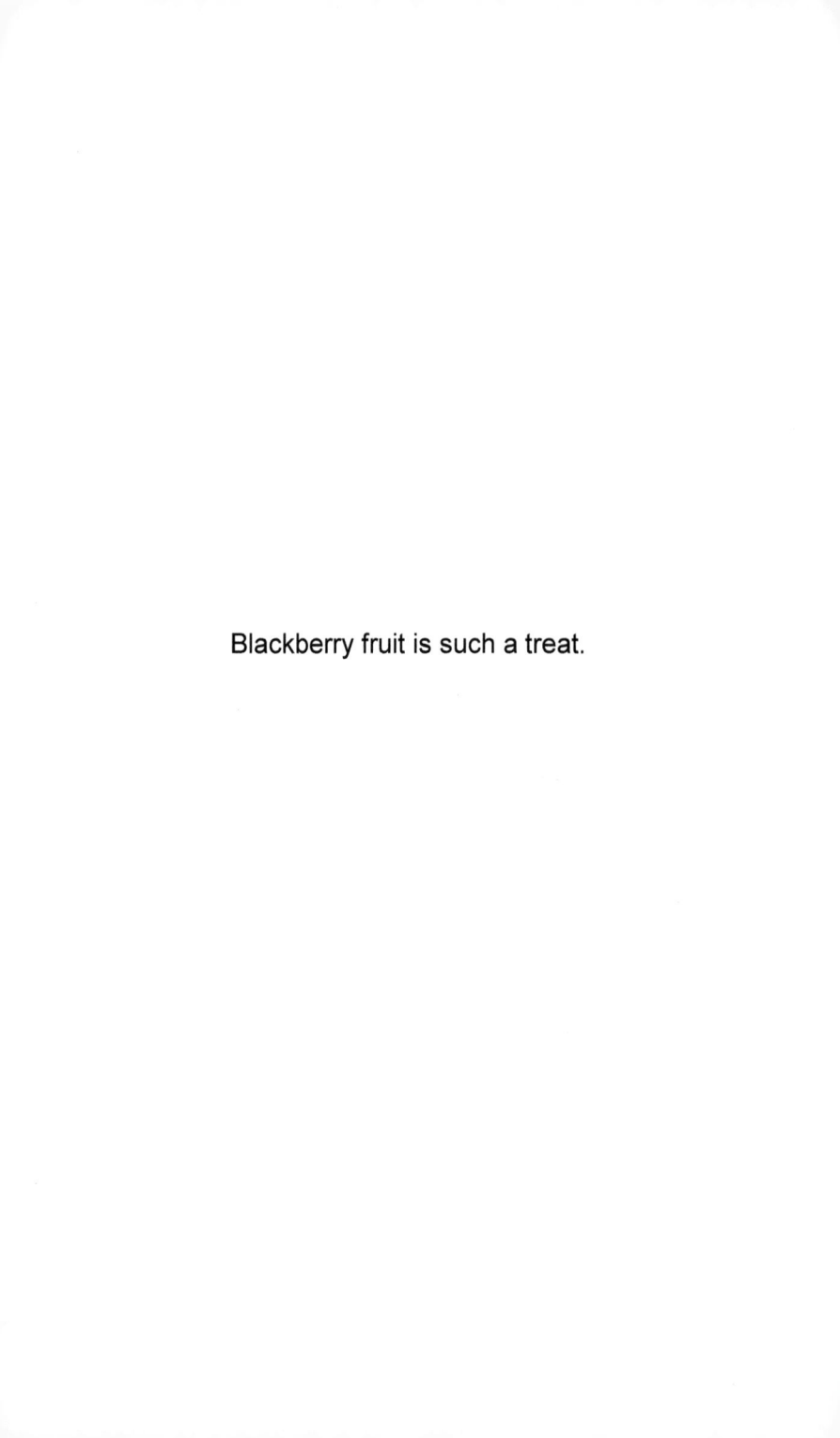

Blackberry fruit is such a treat.

In pies and jams, it loves to play,

But fresh from the vine is the best way!

We pop them in, one by one,

Eating Blackberries is so much fun.

It's Time to Eat a
Blackberry

They grow in patches, big and wide,

In forests green, they love to hide.

We pick and munch with happy cheer,

Blackberry season is finally here!

Their color is dark, almost like night,

But their taste is bright, a pure delight.

With every bite, we feel so strong,

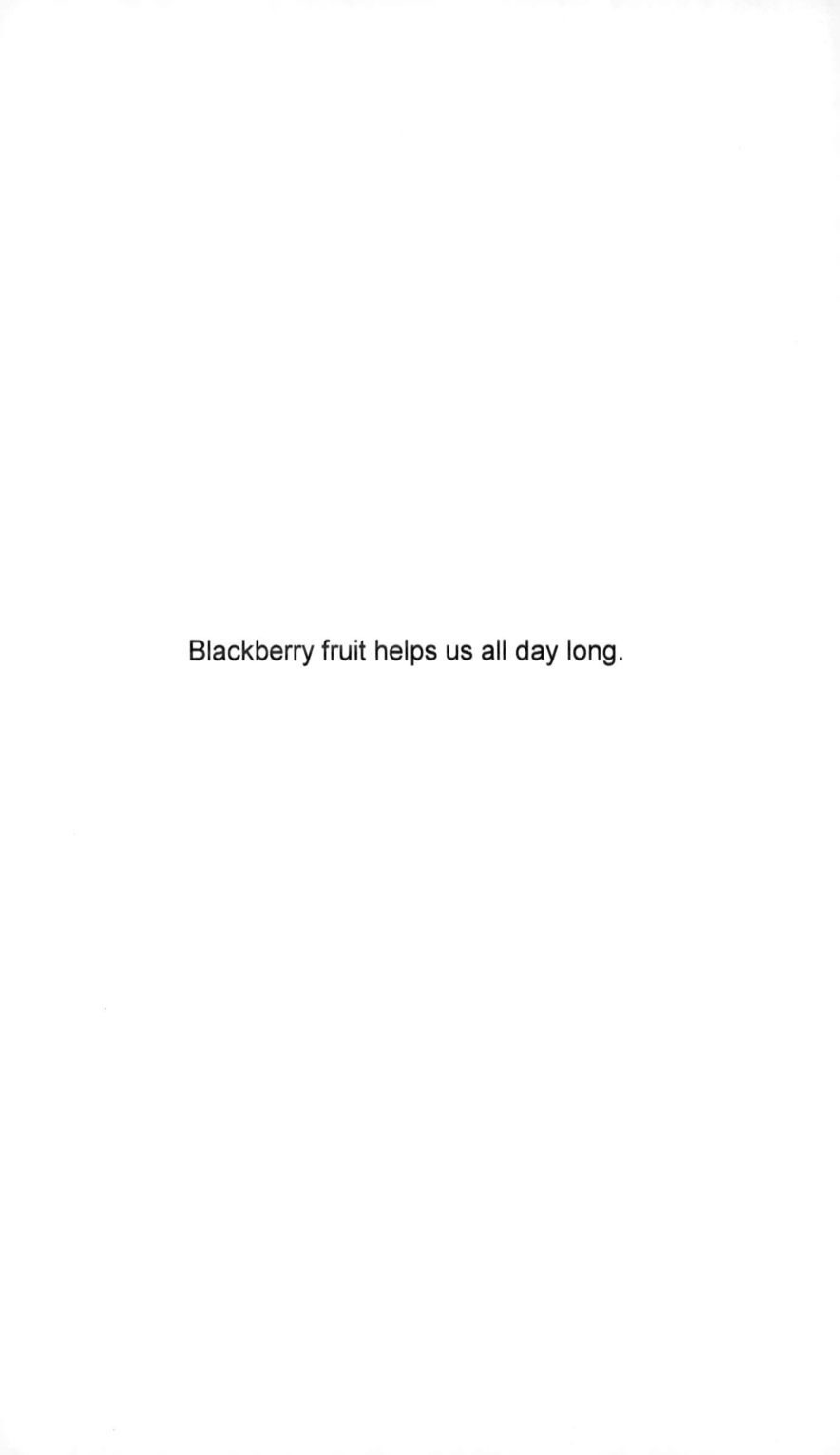

Blackberry fruit helps us all day long.

Some like them raw, some in a pie,

Either way, they make us sigh.

Their juicy goodness fills us up,

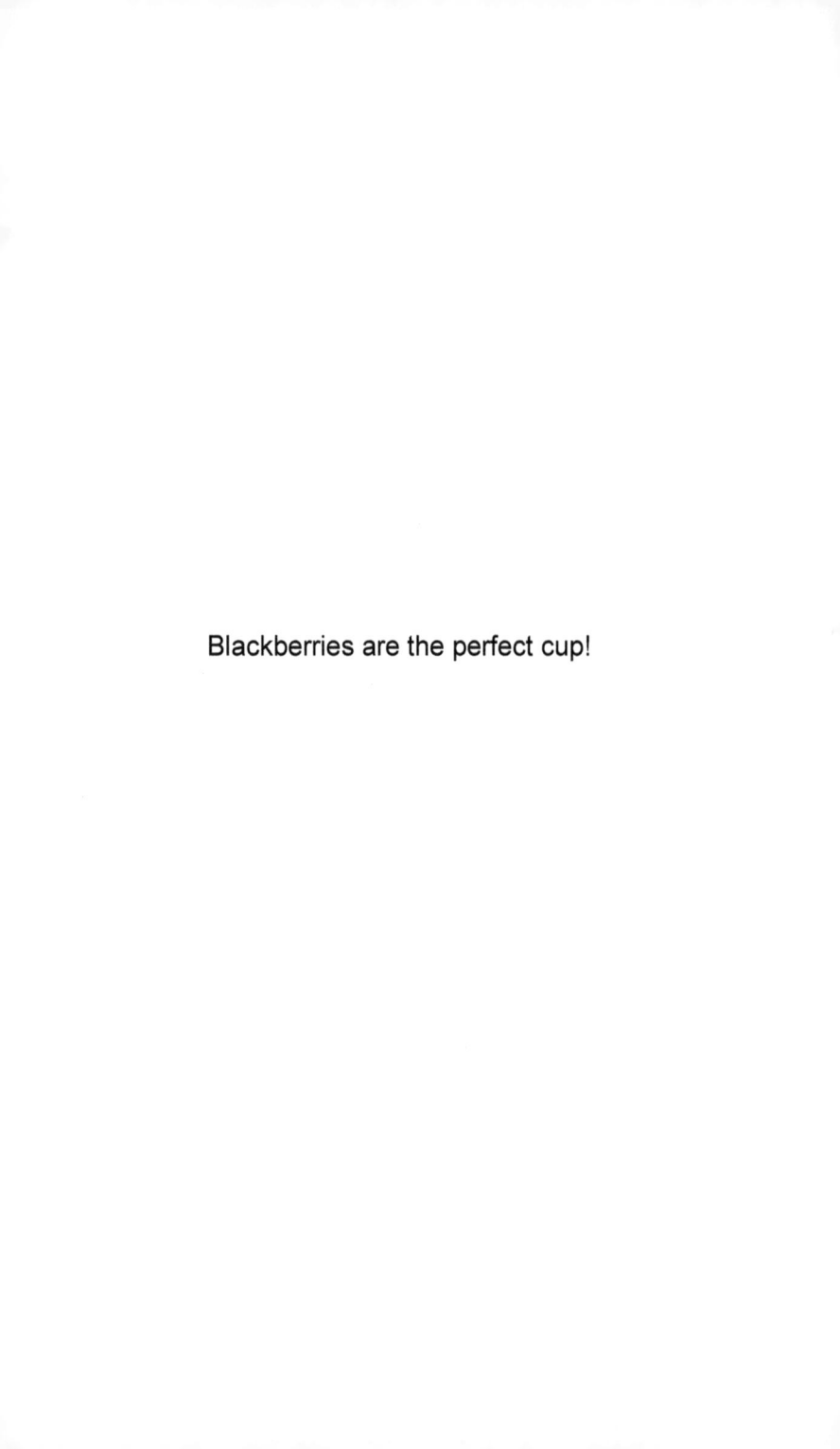

Blackberries are the perfect cup!

They're soft and squishy, but oh so nice,

We love them plain or mixed with ice!

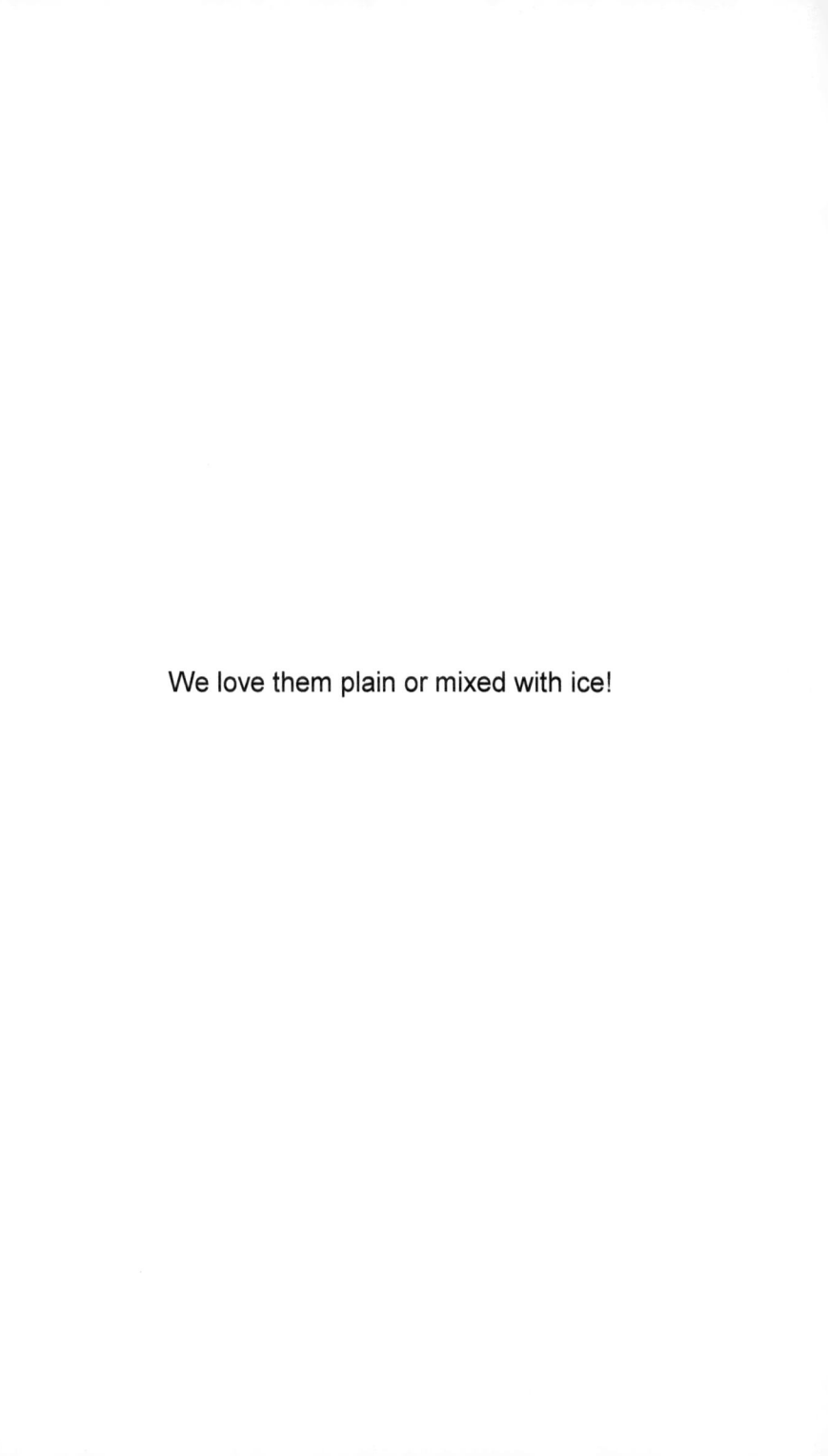

In smoothies cool or snacks to share,

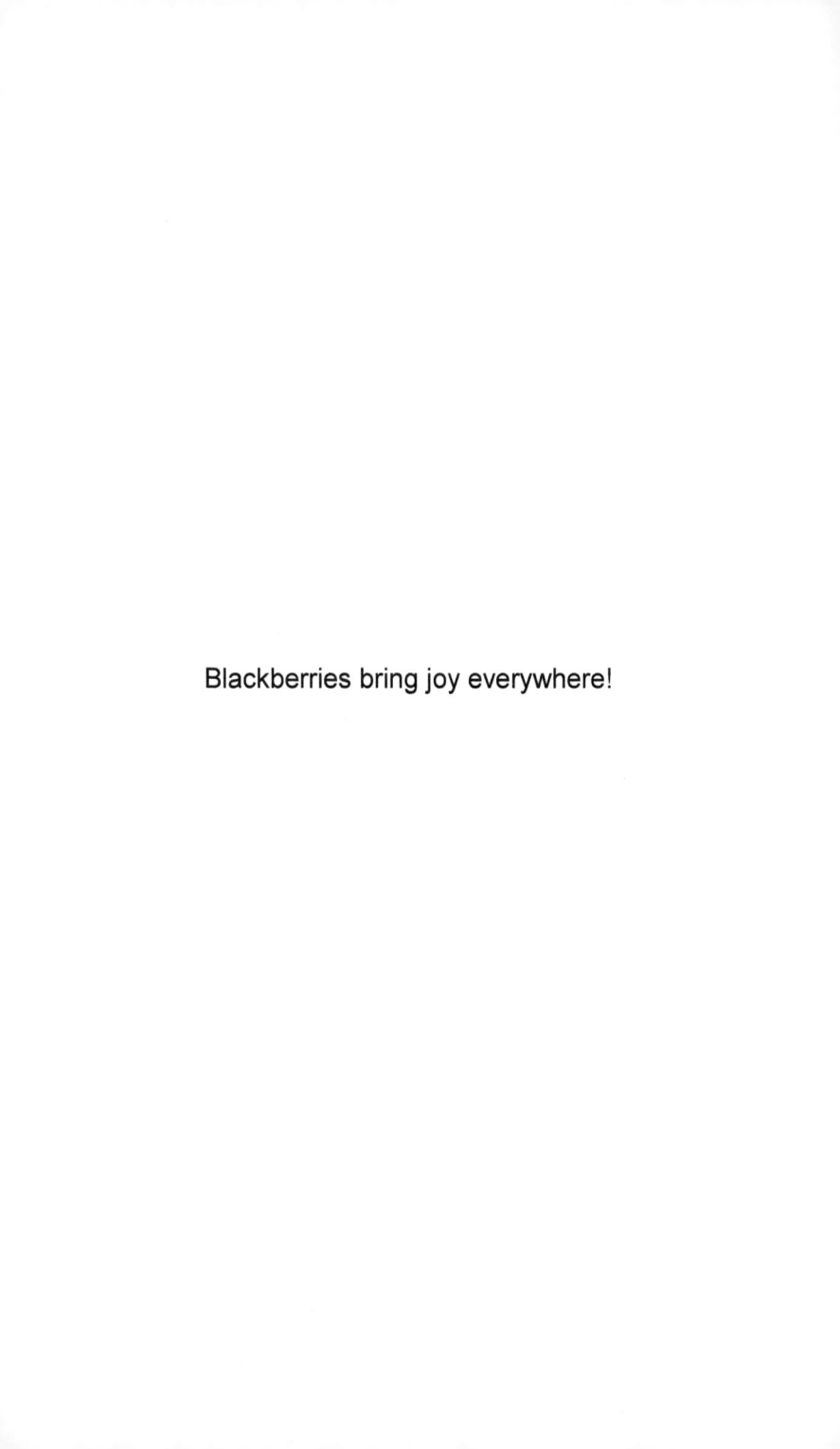

Blackberries bring joy everywhere!

A handful here, a handful there,

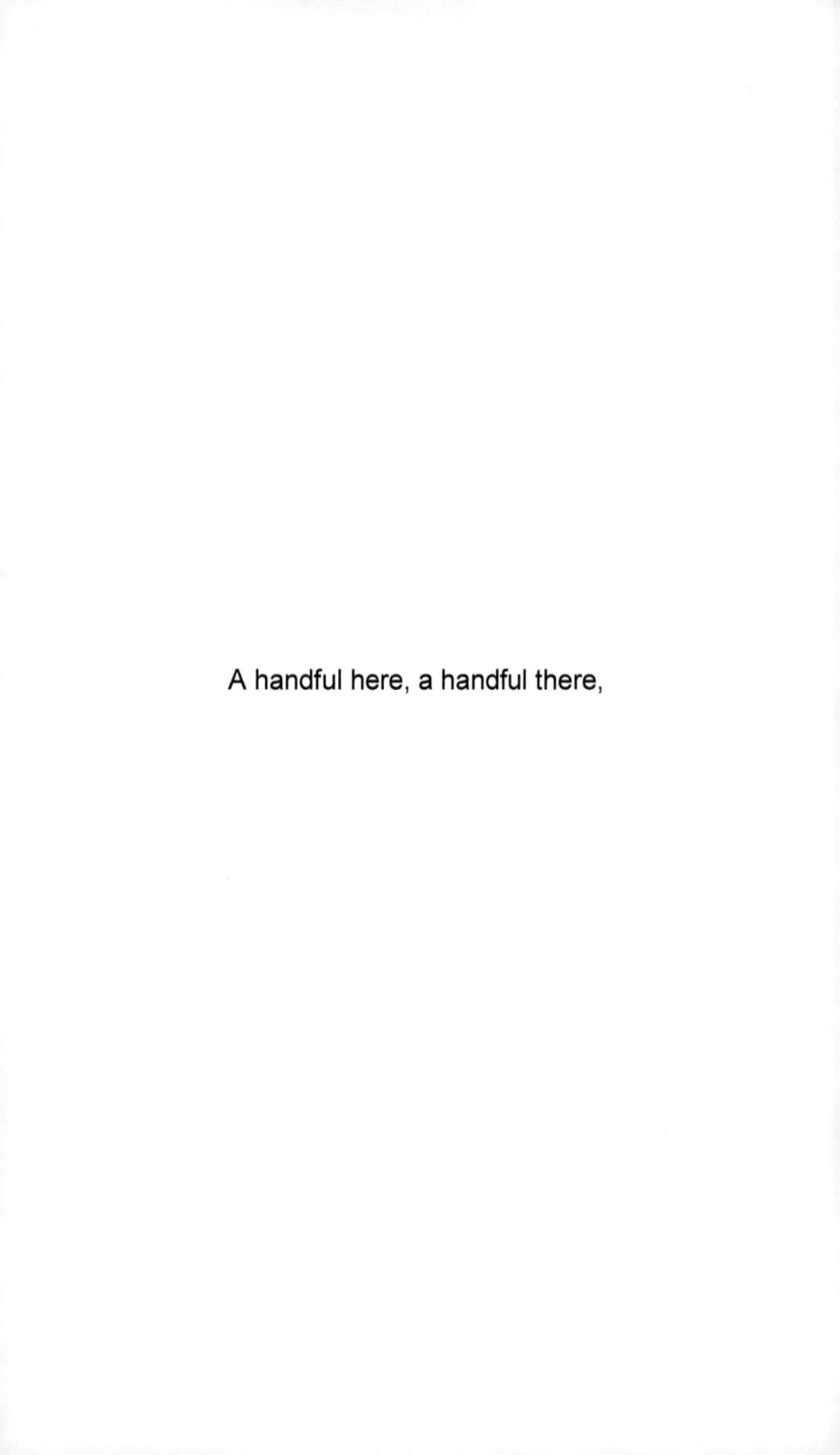

Blackberries bring love everywhere!

They give us energy to jump and play,

It's Time to Eat a
Blackberry

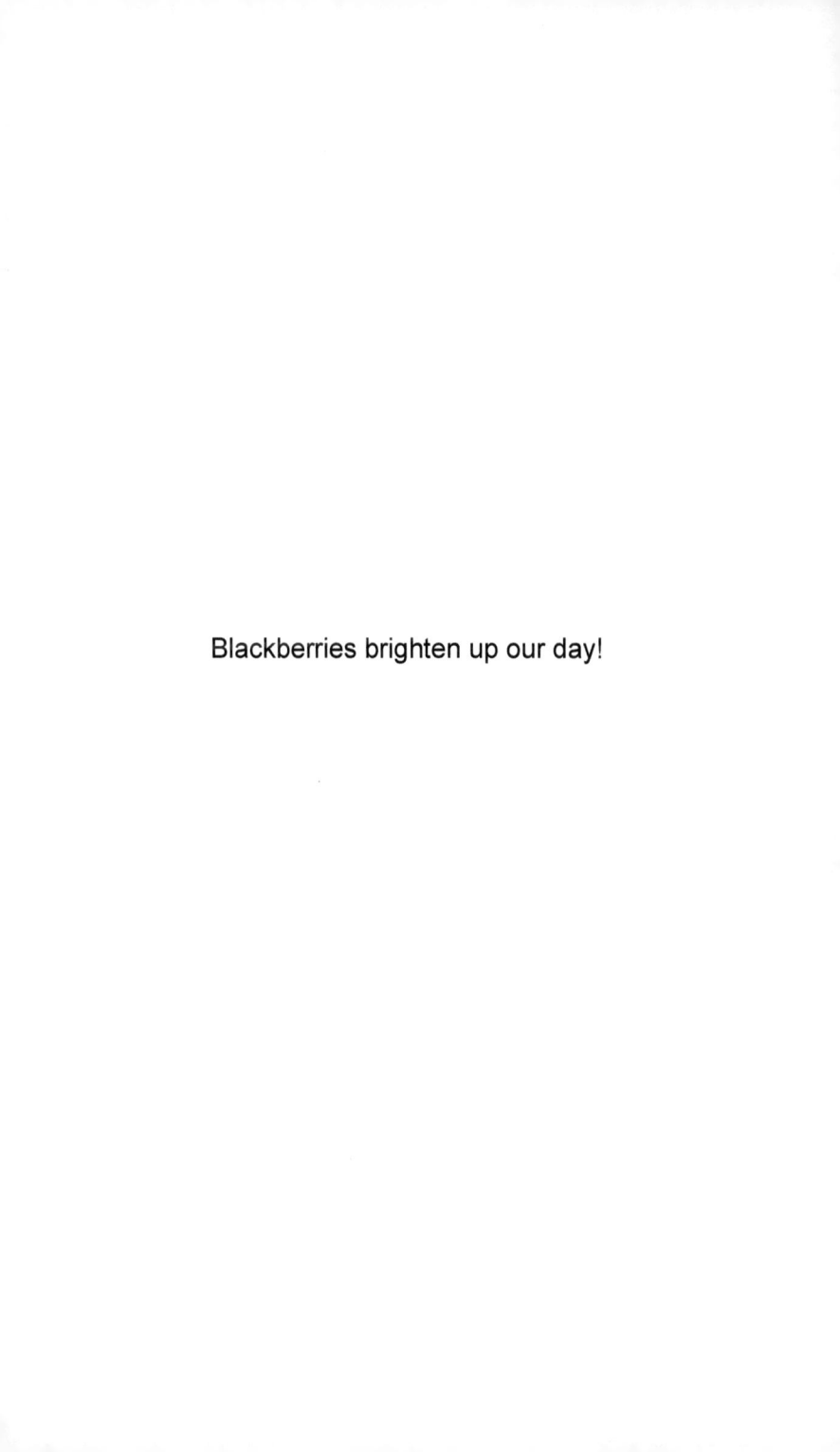

Blackberries brighten up our day!

In salads fresh or on a cake,

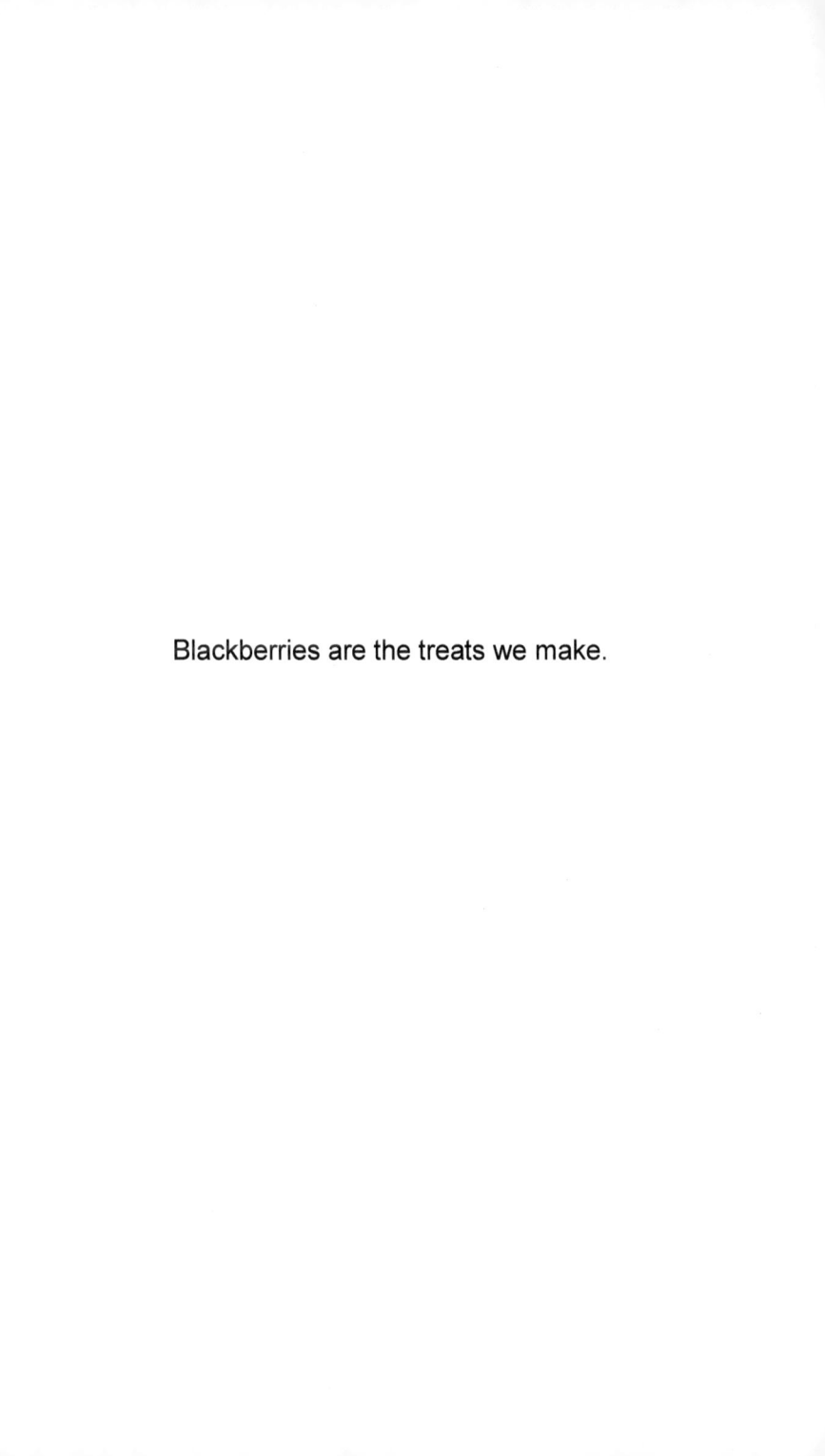

Blackberries are the treats we make.

But eating them plain, straight from the vine,

Is Blackberry time, so sweet and fine!

ABOUT THE CREATOR

Walter the Educator is one of the pseudonyms for Walter Anderson. Formally educated in Chemistry, Business, and Education, he is an educator, an author, a diverse entrepreneur, and he is the son of a disabled war veteran. "Walter the Educator" shares his time between educating and creating. He holds interests and owns several creative projects that entertain, enlighten, enhance, and educate, hoping to inspire and motivate you. Follow, find new works, and stay up to date with Walter the Educator™ at WaltertheEducator.com

Milton Keynes UK
Ingram Content Group UK Ltd.
UKHW020109181024
449757UK00012B/752